Stay Cool!

Be Organized at School!

Student Planner

Activinotes

Activinotes

DAILY JOURNALS, PLANNERS, NOTEBOOKS AND OTHER BLANK BOOKS

Assignments

_____
_____
_____
_____
_____
_____
_____
_____
_____
_____
_____
_____
_____

Quiz & Exams
Schedule :

_____
_____
_____
_____
_____
_____
_____
_____
_____
_____
_____
_____

| Name: | Age: | | School Level: |

Day/Time	Subject	Activities	Description

To do list

Notes

Assignments

_____

Quiz & Exams Schedule :

Name:	Age:	School Level:

Day/Time	Subject	Activities	Description

To do list

Notes

Assignments

Quiz & Exams
Schedule :

| Name: | | Age: | | School Level: |

Day / Time	Subject	Activities	Description

To do list

Notes

Assignments

_____
_____
_____
_____
_____
_____
_____
_____
_____
_____
_____
_____
_____
_____

Quiz & Exams
Schedule :

_____
_____
_____
_____
_____
_____
_____
_____
_____
_____
_____
_____

Name:	Age:		School Level:

Day/Time	Subject	Activities	Description

To do list

Notes

Assignments

Quiz & Exams
Schedule :

Day/Time	Subject	Activities	Description

To do list

Notes

Assignments

_____
_____
_____
_____
_____
_____
_____
_____
_____
_____
_____
_____
_____
_____

Quiz & Exams
Schedule :

_____
_____
_____
_____
_____
_____
_____
_____
_____
_____
_____

Day/Time	Subject	Activities	Description

To do list

Notes

Assignments

_____
_____
_____
_____
_____
_____
_____
_____
_____
_____
_____
_____
_____
_____
_____

**Quiz & Exams
Schedule :**

_____
_____
_____
_____
_____
_____
_____
_____
_____
_____
_____

Name:		Age:		School Level:

Day/Time	Subject	Activities	Description

To do list

Notes

Assignments

_____

_____

_____

_____

_____

_____

_____

_____

_____

_____

_____

_____

_____

Quiz & Exams
Schedule :

_____

_____

_____

_____

_____

_____

_____

_____

_____

_____

_____

_____

Name: **Age:**   **School Level:**

Day / Time	Subject	Activities	Description

To do list

Notes

Assignments

Quiz & Exams Schedule :

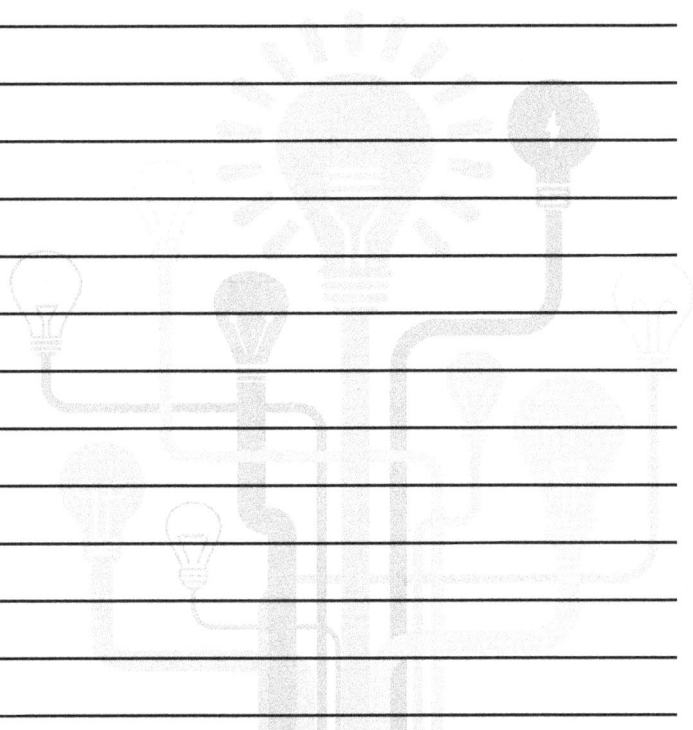

Day/Time	Subject	Activities	Description

To do list

Notes

Assignments

_____
_____
_____
_____
_____
_____
_____
_____
_____
_____
_____
_____
_____
_____

Quiz & Exams
Schedule :

_____
_____
_____
_____
_____
_____
_____
_____
_____
_____
_____

Name:		Age:		School Level:

Day / Time	Subject	Activities	Description

To do list

Notes

Assignments

**Quiz & Exams
Schedule :**

Name:		Age:		School Level:	

Day / Time	Subject	Activities	Description

To do list

Notes

Assignments

Quiz & Exams Schedule :

Day/Time	Subject	Activities	Description

To do list

Notes

Assignments

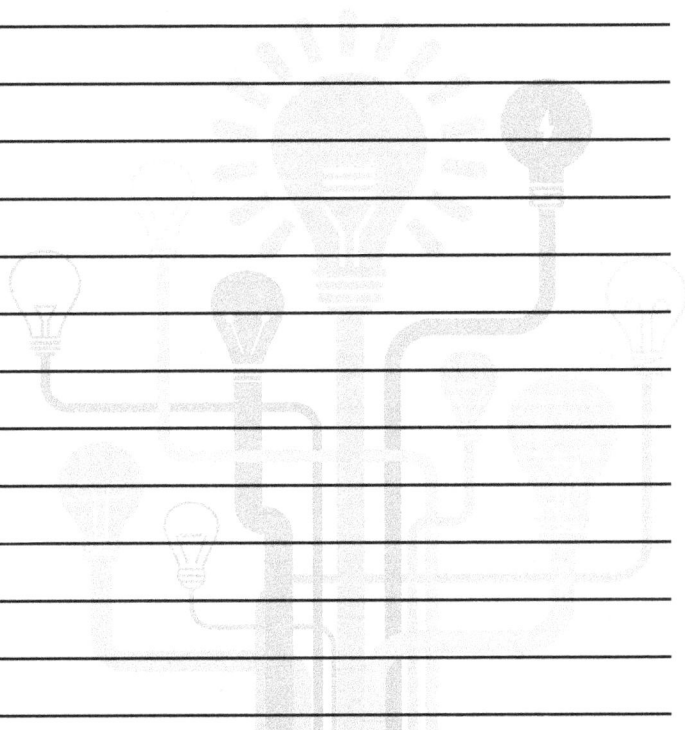

Quiz & Exams
Schedule :

Name: **Age:**   **School Level:**

Day/Time	Subject	Activities	Description

Notes

To do list

Assignments

Quiz & Exams
Schedule :

| Name: | | Age: | | School Level: |

Day / Time	Subject	Activities	Description

To do list

Notes

Assignments

_____
_____
_____
_____
_____
_____
_____
_____
_____
_____
_____
_____
_____

Quiz & Exams Schedule :

_____
_____
_____
_____
_____
_____
_____
_____
_____
_____
_____

Day / Time	Subject	Activities	Description

To do list

Notes

Assignments

Quiz & Exams Schedule :

Day/Time	Subject	Activities	Description

To do list

Notes

Assignments

_____
_____
_____
_____
_____
_____
_____
_____
_____
_____
_____
_____
_____
_____

Quiz & Exams Schedule :

_____
_____
_____
_____
_____
_____
_____
_____
_____
_____
_____
_____

Day/Time	Subject	Activities	Description

To do list

Notes

Assignments

_____
_____
_____
_____
_____
_____
_____
_____
_____
_____
_____
_____
_____
_____
_____
_____
_____

Quiz & Exams
Schedule :

_____
_____
_____
_____
_____
_____
_____
_____
_____
_____
_____

Name:	Age:	School Level:

Day / Time	Subject	Activities	Description

To do list

Notes

Assignments

_____
_____
_____
_____
_____
_____
_____
_____
_____
_____
_____
_____
_____
_____
_____

Quiz & Exams Schedule :

_____
_____
_____
_____
_____
_____
_____
_____
_____
_____
_____
_____
_____

Day / Time	Subject	Activities	Description

To do list

Notes

Assignments

_____

_____

_____

_____

_____

_____

_____

_____

_____

_____

_____

_____

Quiz & Exams
Schedule :

_____

_____

_____

_____

_____

_____

_____

_____

_____

_____

_____

Day / Time	Subject	Activities	Description

To do list

Notes

Assignments

Quiz & Exams Schedule :

| Name: | Age: | School Level: |

Day / Time	Subject	Activities	Description

To do list

Notes

Assignments

_____
_____
_____
_____
_____
_____
_____
_____
_____
_____
_____
_____
_____
_____
_____

Quiz & Exams
Schedule :

_____
_____
_____
_____
_____
_____
_____
_____
_____
_____

Name: **Age:**   **School Level:**

Day / Time	Subject	Activities	Description

To do list

Notes

Assignments

Quiz & Exams Schedule :

Day / Time	Subject	Activities	Description

To do list

Notes

Assignments

Quiz & Exams
Schedule :

Day / Time	Subject	Activities	Description

To do list

Notes

Assignments

_____
_____
_____
_____
_____
_____
_____
_____
_____
_____
_____
_____
_____
_____

Quiz & Exams Schedule :

_____
_____
_____
_____
_____
_____
_____
_____
_____
_____

Day/Time	Subject	Activities	Description

To do list

Notes

Assignments

_____
_____
_____
_____
_____
_____
_____
_____
_____
_____
_____
_____
_____
_____

Quiz & Exams Schedule :

_____
_____
_____
_____
_____
_____
_____
_____
_____
_____

Name: **Age:**   **School Level:**

Day / Time	Subject	Activities	Description

Notes

To do list

Assignments

_____

Quiz & Exams
Schedule :

Day/Time	Subject	Activities	Description

To do list

Notes

Assignments

_____
_____
_____
_____
_____
_____
_____
_____
_____
_____
_____
_____
_____
_____

Quiz & Exams
Schedule :

_____
_____
_____
_____
_____
_____
_____
_____
_____
_____
_____
_____

Day / Time	Subject	Activities	Description

To do list

Notes

Assignments

Quiz & Exams Schedule :

Day / Time	Subject	Activities	Description

To do list

Notes

Assignments

Quiz & Exams
Schedule :

Name:		Age:		School Level:	

Day / Time	Subject	Activities	Description

To do list

Notes

Assignments

_____
_____
_____
_____
_____
_____
_____
_____
_____
_____
_____
_____
_____
_____
_____
_____

Quiz & Exams Schedule :

_____
_____
_____
_____
_____
_____
_____
_____
_____
_____
_____
_____
_____

Day / Time	Subject	Activities	Description

To do list

Notes

Assignments

Quiz & Exams
Schedule :

Name: **Age:**   **School Level:**

Day / Time	Subject	Activities	Description

Notes

To do list

Assignments

Quiz & Exams
Schedule :

Name:		Age:		School Level:

Day/Time	Subject	Activities	Description

To do list

Notes

Assignments

_____
_____
_____
_____
_____
_____
_____
_____
_____
_____
_____
_____
_____

Quiz & Exams
Schedule :

_____
_____
_____
_____
_____
_____
_____
_____
_____
_____
_____

Day/Time	Subject	Activities	Description

To do list

Notes

Assignments

Quiz & Exams
Schedule :

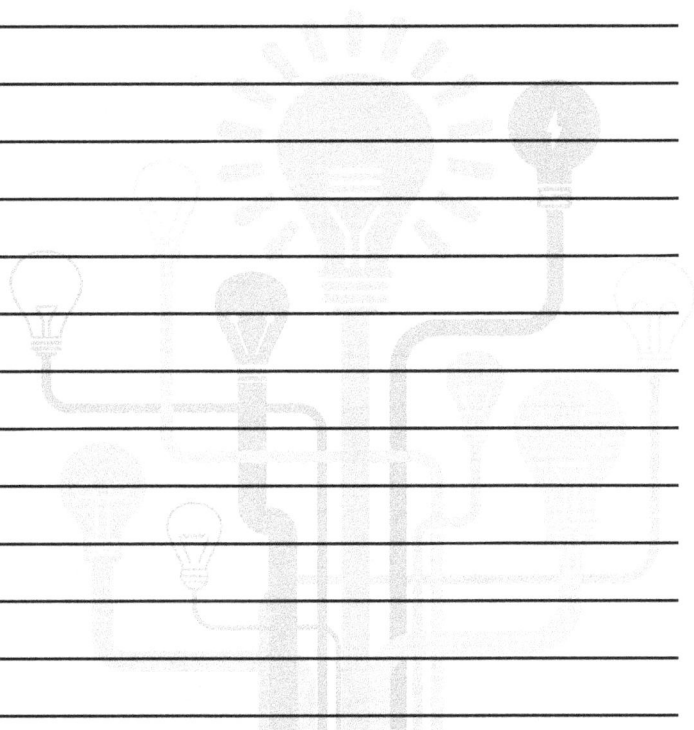

Name:		Age:		School Level:

Day / Time	Subject	Activities	Description

To do list

Notes

Assignments

_____
_____
_____
_____
_____
_____
_____
_____
_____
_____
_____
_____
_____
_____

Quiz & Exams
Schedule :

_____
_____
_____
_____
_____
_____
_____
_____
_____
_____

Day/Time	Subject	Activities	Description

To do list

Notes

Assignments

Quiz & Exams Schedule :

Day / Time	Subject	Activities	Description

To do list

Notes

Assignments

Quiz & Exams
Schedule :

Day / Time	Subject	Activities	Description

To do list

Notes

Assignments

Quiz & Exams Schedule :

Day / Time	Subject	Activities	Description

To do list

Notes

Assignments

Quiz & Exams Schedule :

Day/Time	Subject	Activities	Description

To do list

Notes

Assignments

_____
_____
_____
_____
_____
_____
_____
_____
_____
_____
_____
_____
_____
_____

Quiz & Exams
Schedule :

_____
_____
_____
_____
_____
_____
_____
_____
_____
_____
_____
_____
_____

Name:	Age:		School Level:

Day / Time	Subject	Activities	Description

To do list

Notes

Assignments

_____
_____
_____
_____
_____
_____
_____
_____
_____
_____
_____
_____

Quiz & Exams
Schedule :

_____
_____
_____
_____
_____
_____
_____
_____
_____
_____
_____

| Name: | Age: | School Level: |

Day/Time	Subject	Activities	Description

To do list

Notes

Assignments

Quiz & Exams Schedule :

Day / Time	Subject	Activities	Description

To do list

Notes

Assignments

_____
_____
_____
_____
_____
_____
_____
_____
_____
_____
_____
_____
_____
_____
_____
_____

Quiz & Exams
Schedule :

_____
_____
_____
_____
_____
_____
_____
_____
_____
_____
_____
_____
_____

| Name: | Age: | | School Level: |

Day/Time	Subject	Activities	Description

To do list

Notes

Assignments

_____
_____
_____
_____
_____
_____
_____
_____
_____
_____
_____
_____
_____
_____

Quiz & Exams Schedule :

_____
_____
_____
_____
_____
_____
_____
_____
_____
_____

Name:		Age:		School Level:	

Day / Time	Subject	Activities	Description

To do list

Notes

Assignments

_____
_____
_____
_____
_____
_____
_____
_____
_____
_____
_____
_____
_____
_____

Quiz & Exams Schedule :

_____
_____
_____
_____
_____
_____
_____
_____
_____
_____
_____
_____

Day/Time	Subject	Activities	Description

To do list

Notes

Assignments

_____
_____
_____
_____
_____
_____
_____
_____
_____
_____
_____
_____
_____
_____

Quiz & Exams
Schedule :

_____
_____
_____
_____
_____
_____
_____
_____
_____
_____
_____

Day/Time	Subject	Activities	Description

To do list

Notes

Assignments

_____
_____
_____
_____
_____
_____
_____
_____
_____
_____
_____
_____
_____
_____
_____
_____

Quiz & Exams Schedule :

_____
_____
_____
_____
_____
_____
_____
_____
_____
_____
_____

Name:	Age:		School Level:

Day / Time	Subject	Activities	Description

Notes

To do list

Assignments

Quiz & Exams Schedule :

Day / Time	Subject	Activities	Description

To do list

Notes

Assignments

Quiz & Exams
Schedule :

Name:	Age:		School Level:

Day / Time	Subject	Activities	Description

To do list

Notes

Assignments

_____
_____
_____
_____
_____
_____
_____
_____
_____
_____
_____
_____
_____
_____

Quiz & Exams
Schedule :

_____
_____
_____
_____
_____
_____
_____
_____
_____
_____
_____

| Name: | | Age: | | School Level: |

Name: | **Age:** | **School Level:**

Day / Time	Subject	Activities	Description

Notes

To do list

Assignments

Quiz & Exams
Schedule :

www.ingramcontent.com/pod-product-compliance
Lightning Source LLC
Chambersburg PA
CBHW081336090426

42737CB00017B/3171